LEARNING TO READ

Masha Bell believes that education bestows great advantages and that an educated population is an essential ingredient of a healthy modern society and democracy. She is therefore passionately interested in enabling as many people as possible to read and write effectively.

Since having to stop teaching English and modern languages on health grounds in 1994, she has devoted nearly all of her time and energy to understanding why so many English-speaking children have literacy problems, and how they can be helped to overcome them.

Her comparatively late introduction to English at the age of 14 has made her exceptionally aware of its learning problems.

By the same author

Understanding English Spelling
Published in 2004 (Pegasus Educational)
ISBN 190349012x

HOW TO USE THIS BOOK

The book aims to teach the main sounds (not the names) for all letters except q, followed by the 36 most often used letters strings, like ck, qu, ch, tch and sh, in the order shown on the Contents page.

With pupils who are not complete beginners, the Contents page can be used to assess what they already know. Any gaps in their knowledge of letter sounds can then be filled by turning to the relevant page.

Beginners should be taught to sound out the letters for the key words shown on the even pages (on the left) and to blend them into words, and to practise doing the same for other words on the odd pages opposite.

All key words are carried forward at the top of the odd pages, and letters at the bottom, for revision and for helping with the decoding of new words. If children are encouraged to learn to spell as well as read the basic letter sounds, they will memorise them with greater certainty.

No pupil should be pushed ahead until the earlier letter sounds have been thoroughly learned. Short, regular sessions of 5-10 minutes are more effective than intermittent longer ones.

The website www.englishspellingproblems.co.uk provides more words for learning to read the basic English spelling patterns which this book teaches pupils to decode.

This book teaches children how to read. They are more likely to want to learn this skill if they are regularly read to.

Masha Bell

LEARNING TO READ

letter sounds
and
common tricky words

PEGASUS EDUCATIONAL

PEGASUS EDUCATIONAL

A CIP catalogue record for this title is
available from the British Library

ISBN 13:-978-1-903490-23-5

Pegasus Educational is an imprint of
Pegasus Elliot MacKenzie Publishers Ltd.
www.pegasuspublishers.com

First published in 2007

Pegasus
Sheraton House Castle Park
Cambridge England

Contents

61 basic spellings for English sounds

Tricky letters and words

c a t   **h** a t

cat   h a t

cat
at
hat

d o g   **b a g**

c a t
h a t

d o g   **b** a **g**

d **o** t	**b** a d
g **o** t	d a d
c **o** t	h a d
h **o** t	a

Dad had a bad hot dog.

b	c	d	g	h	t	a	o
B	C	D	G	H	T	A	O

9

s u n   b e d

cat hat **bag do**g

sun   be**d**

u s	**n e** t	**s** a t	o **n**
b **u s**	**s e** t	**s** a d	**n** o t
b **u n**	g **e** t	c a **n**	**n** o d
n u t		a **n**	
c **u** t		a **n** d	
h **u** t		**s** a **n** d	

A cat sat on a sun bed
and got hot.

b	c	d	g	h	**n**	**s**	t		a	**e**	o	**u**
B	C	D	G	H	**N**	**S**	T		A	**E**	O	**U**

l i p s   m u g

b a g   **cat**
d o g   **h** at

b e d   **s u n**

l i **p** s   **m** u g

s **i p**	**p** o **p**	**m** u **m**
s **l i p**	**p l** o **p**	**m** u d
p i t	**p** o t	
d **i** g s **i** t **i** n **i** t	**p** e n **p** e t	**m** a t **p** a t l a **p**

M u m d u g a s a n d p i t a n d
m u m ' s p e t h e n g o t i n i t.

b c d g h **l** **m** n **p** s t	a e **i** o u
B C D G H **L** **M** N **P** S T	A E **I** O U

f o x

j u g

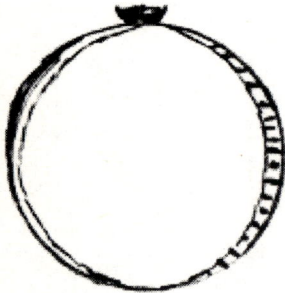

r i n g

c a r

	b **e** d	**s** **u** n	
		m u g	
h a t	**b** a **g**		
c a t	**d** o g	**l** i **p** s	

f o **x**	**j** u g	**r** i n g	c **ar**
b o **x**	**j** o g	**r** a t	**f** **ar**
f i **x**	**j** o t	**r** a n	j **ar**
m i **x**	**j** o b		st **ar**
s i **x**		**r** u b	sc **ar**
	j a b	**r** u g	
f i t	**j** a m		**ar** m
f a t		br i n g	**f** **ar** m
f e d		str i n g	
f o g			
f u n			

A car hit a fat fox in fog. It did not get far.

Dad had a job on a farm and

got a bad cut on his arm.

b	c	d	**f**	g	h	**j**	l	m	n	p	**r**	s	t	**x**	a	e	i	o	u
B	C	D	**F**	G	H	**J**	L	M	N	P	**R**	S	T	**X**	A	E	I	O	U

cat **h**at **bag** bed   **sun** **m**ug jug   **lips** ring **car**   **do**g fox

Blends in ends and starts

nd	nt	mp	ng	fl	cl gl	sl
a**nd**		ca**mp**	ba**ng**	**fl**ap	**cl**ap	**sl**am
ba**nd**		la**mp**	ha**ng**	**fl**ip	**cl**ip	
ha**nd**			ra**ng**	**fl**op	**cl**op	**sl**ip
sa**nd**		cla**mp**	sa**ng**			**sl**ing
				flat		
e**nd**		cra**mp**	si**ng**	**fl**ag	**gl**ad	**sl**ot
be**nd**	be**nt**					
le**nd**	le**nt**	sta**mp**	so**ng**			
se**nd**	se**nt**		lo**ng**			

Jan rang dad on camp.

Ted had cramp.

Ned bent a tent peg.

Pip sang lots of songs.

Jim lent him a hand.

b c d f g h j l m n p r s t x a e i o u
B C D F G H J L M N P R S T X A E I O U

cat hat **bag** bed **do**g fox **sun m**ug jug **lip**s **r**ing **c**ar

Blends in starts and ends

br	dr		st		sp	spr
cr						
fr	**tr**					**str**
gr						

br	dr		st		sp	spr
bring	**dr**ag	**st**ep	ne**st**	mu**st**	**sp**it	**spr**ing
	drink		pe**st**	ju**st**	**sp**at	**spr**int
crab		**st**op	re**st**	du**st**	**sp**ot	
	trap			ru**st**		**str**ip
from	**tr**ip	**st**and		cru**st**	**sp**end	**str**ap
			fi**st**		**sp**ent	
grab			li**st**	lo**st**		**str**ong
			mi**st**			**str**ing

Jen did not bring strong string.

Pam's armband got lost.

Tom got lots of spots and must rest.

b	c	d	f	g	h	j	l	m	n	p	r	s	t	x		a	e	i	o	u
B	C	D	F	G	H	J	L	M	N	P	R	S	T	X		A	E	I	O	U

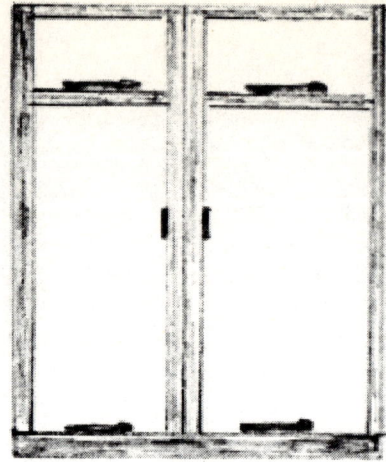

v a n   **w i n d o w**

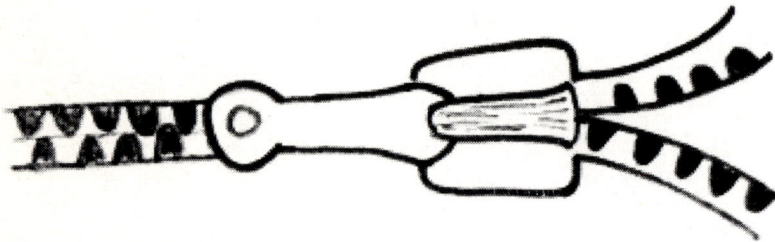

z i p

cat hat bag   dog fox   sun mug   bed   lips
car   jug   ring

v an   **w** ind **ow**   **z** ip

vet	**w**ind	**z**ap
	wish	
vest		bu**zz**
	wet	
	went	qui**z**
	wing	is = iz
	s**w**ing	his = hiz
	s**w**im	
		as = az
	elb**ow**	has = haz

Singing and swinging on his swing,

Sam fell off and cut his elbow.

b	c	d	f	g	h	j	l	m	n	p	r	s	t	**v**	**w**	x	**z**	a	e	i	o	u
B	C	D	F	G	H	J	L	M	N	P	R	S	T	**V**	**W**	X	**Z**	A	E	I	O	U

fish

chair

patch

cat hat **bag** van   bed   li**p**s **z**ip ring   **do**g fox   sun **m**ug jug
car   wind**ow**

fi **sh**   **ch air**   pa **tch**

di**sh**	**sh**ip	**ch**at	ca**tch**
	shop		ma**tch**
ma**sh**		**ch**in	sna**tch**
ra**sh**	**sh**ut	**ch**ip	scra**tch**
cra**sh**		**ch**op	
spla**sh**	**sh**elf	**ch**ap	i**tch**
			di**tch**
hu**sh**	**sh**in	**air**	
ru**sh**		h**air**	ri**ch**
bru**sh**	**sh**ort	f**air**	mu**ch**
cru**sh**	**sh**rug	p**air**	su**ch**

Fred had a dish of mash and fresh fish.

Dad got a bad scratch at a match.

Mum got a pair of chairs at a fair.

b	c	d	f	g	h	j	l	m	n	p	r	s	t	v	w	x	z		a	e	i	o	u
B	C	D	F	G	H	J	L	M	N	P	R	S	T	V	W	X	Z		A	E	I	O	U

3

||||

three

cat hat **bag** van   bed   li**p**s ring **z**ip   dog fox   **s**un **m**ug **j**ug

car   chair pa**tch**   fi**sh**   win**d**ow

th r **ee**   **th**is   **th**ing

teeth deep	the thin
sleep	think
tree sheep	then thick
see	them
bee sheet	thank
	than
sweet	that

A sheep that got buzzed by bees ran under a tree.
[buzd]
Then it fell asleep.

Jan fell from a tree and lost three teeth.

b	c	d	f	g	**h**	j	l	m	n	p	r	s	**t**	v	w	x	z	a	e	i	o	u
B	C	D	F	G	**H**	J	L	M	N	P	R	S	**T**	V	W	X	Z	A	E	I	O	U

king **qu ee n**

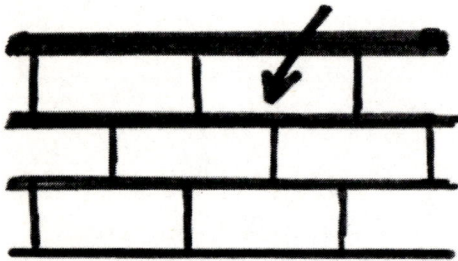

brick

cat hat bag van   bed   lips ring zip   dog fox   sun mug jug

car   chair patch   three   fish   window

k i n g   **q u** ee n   b r i **c k**

kid	**qu**it	ki**ck**	pe**ck**
kit		si**ck**	ne**ck**
	quilt	sti**ck**	
kept		**qu**i**ck**	**qu**a**ck**
keep		lo**ck**	du**ck**
		blo**ck**	mu**ck**
chee**k**		clo**ck**	stu**ck**
		so**ck**	

Mad King Ken keeps dogs and ducks

and locks his socks in a big black box.

His ducks quack a lot and get stuck in muck.

His dogs lick the cheeks of Queen Cathleen.

The queen is not keen on that.

b c d f g h j **k** l m n p **q** r s t v w x z   a e i o u

B C D F G H J **K** L M N P **Q** R S T V W X Z   A E I O U

yes

dummy

five

fly

cat hat bag van   bed   lips ring zip   dog fox   sun
mug jug

car chair patch   three queen   king brick fish window

y es	du mm y	fl y	f i v e
yet	yummy	by	dive
	mummy	my	drive
yap	tummy	sky	
			bike
	funny	try	
	runny	dry	ride
		cry	hide
	happy	shy	side
	hippy	fry	

My mum likes her bike. My dad likes red wine.

I like a hike with my dog by my side.

I think it's funny if my sister is silly and my mummy

gets cross.

b c d f g h j k l m n p q r s t v w x y z   a e i o u
B C D F G H J K L M N P Q R S T V W X Y Z   A E I O U

cake

chain

tray

cat hat bag van bed lips ring zip dog fox sun mug jug
car chair patch three queen king brick fish window

yes dummy fly five

cake		chain	tray
make	late	rain	say
bake	plate	train	stay
take		pain	spray
	gave		
made	shave	nail	day
		snail	play
game		tail	
name		trail	way
same	shape	wail	sway
	spade	paid	pay

Mum made a cake and we went for a hike by a lake.
[wee]

We ate the cake from paper plates.

Then we played a game and three snails left trails on the plates.

cone

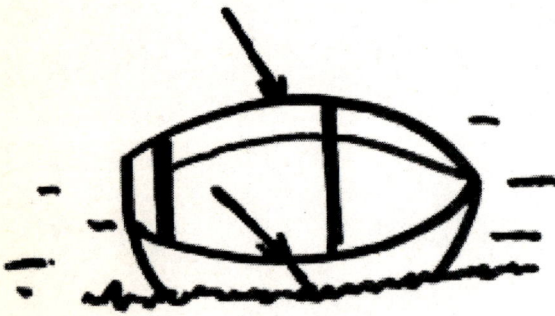

boat

toe

cat hat bag van   bed   lips ring zip   dog fox   sun mug jug
car chair patch   three queen king brick fish window

yes dummy   five   fly
           cake chain   tray

cone   **boat**   **toe**

stone home	goat coach	doe
bone	throat	hoe
rode	road	roe
broke	roast	load	woe
choke rope	toast	loaf	
joke		and: so [soe]
poke pole	oats soap	no
		go
		ago

I like jam on toast and Sunday roast.

I like my dad's jokes.

I like frogs that croak and goats with thick coats.

I had a moan when I trod on a stone as I got off the boat.

31

cube

skewer

cue

cat hat bag van   bed   lips ring zip   dog fox   sun mug jug
window
car chair patch   three queen   king brick fish   dummy   yes

five		fly	
cake	chain	tray	
cone	boat	toe	so

cube   skewer   cue   new

tube	jewels		few
mule	mildew	blue	blew
tune		clue	flew
June		glue	

My sister June has lots of blue cubes

and she can sing quite a few jolly tunes.
[shee]

A week ago a strong wind blew

and few ducks flew

but I had a long ride on a mule.

33

coin

toy

claw

cat **h**at **bag** **v**an   bed   **lip**s **r**ing **z**ip   **dog f**ox   **sun** **m**ug **j**ug
car chair pa**tch**   **three qu**een   **k**ing br**ick**   **fish**   win**d**o**w**
dumm**y**   **y**es

f**i**ve		fl**y**
cake	ch**ai**n	tr**ay**
c**o**ne	b**oa**t	t**oe** s**o**
t**u**be	sk**ew**er	c**ue** n**ew**

c**oi**n   **toy**   cl**aw**

j**oi**n	b**oy**	j**aw**	**or**
j**oi**nt	j**oy**	r**aw**	**for**
p**oi**nt	enj**oy**	dr**aw**	n**or**
oil		str**aw**	
b**oi**l		s**aw**	jigs**aw**
c**oi**l			sees**aw**
s**oi**l		cr**aw**l	
sp**oi**l		spr**aw**l	

My little sister makes silly noises as she plays with her toys.
    [litl]
I like drawing monsters with big jaws or sharp claws.

On Sunday my mum roasts a joint.

My dad likes digging the garden soil.

 **bird**
 **perch**
 **church**

a bird on a perch

cat hat bag van   bed   lips ring zip   dog fox sun mug jug
car chair patch   three queen   king brick fish window
dummy yes

five		fly	
cake	chain	tray	
cone	boat	toe	so
tube	skewer	cue	new

coin	toy	
crawl	claw	or

bird   perch   church

third girl	her	fur nurse
twirl	herb	purse
chirp		burn
dirt	jerk	turn hurt
first skirt		
thirst squirt	serve [serv]	curl turtle
		purple

A cat can make a bird fly off its perch.

My sister spoilt her purple skirt as she twirled a stick
                                        [twirld]
and fell on a patch of dirt but she did not get hurt.

My dad's birthday is on June the first.

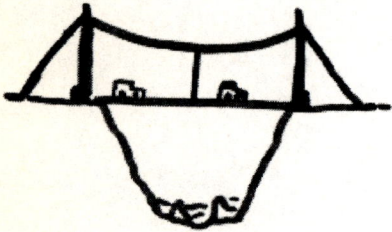

bridge

station

face

cat hat bag van   bed   lips ring zip   dog fox   sun mug jug
car chair patch   three queen   king brick fish window
dummy yes

five		fly	
cake	chain	tray	
cone	boat	toe	so
tube	skewer	cue	new

coin		toy	
crawl		claw	or
bird	perch	church	

bri**dge**   st**ation**   fa**ce**

[**dge** = j]   [**ation** = aishn]   [**ce** = ss]

fri**dge** [frij]	carn**ation** [carn-aishn]	ra**ce**
e**dge**		la**ce**
he**dge**	coron**ation**	
le**dge**		i**ce**
	inform**ation**	ri**ce**
do**dge** [doj]		mi**ce**
fu**dge**	explan**ation**	
nu**dge**		ni**ce**
smu**dge**		spi**ce**

I gave my sister a nudge and she smudged her face with fudge.

My dad gave my mum a nice bunch of carnations as he met her off the train at the railway station.

I am not keen on rice with hot spices.

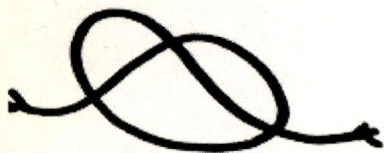

knot

$1 + 1 = 3$ $\underline{X}$

wrong

light

cat hat bag van   bed   lips ring zip   dog fox   sun mug jug
car chair patch   three queen   king brick fish   window
dummy   yes

five		fly	
cake	chain	tray	
cone	boat	toe	so
tube	skewer	cue	new

coin		toy	
crawl		claw	or
bird	perch	church	
bridge	station		face

knot	wrong	light
[kn = n]	[wr = r]	[ight = ite]
knock [nock]	wrist [rist]	fight [fite]
knob	write	might
knee	wrote	night
kneel		right
knife	wrap	tight
knew	wreck	For high say [hy]
		like 'my'

I hurt my knee as I knocked it against my bike.

I write with my left hand but my mum writes with her right.

My sister likes a light by her bed at night.

Birds can fly high in the sky.

Revision test for basic phonics

25 basic letters

an **e**nd **i**n **o**n **u**p

big **c**at **d**og fo**x** **g**ot **h**at **j**ug

king **l**amp **m**ud **n**ut **p**in **r**ed **s**un **t**op

van **w**ind bo**x** **y**es **z**ip

36 basic letter sets

quit **sh**ip **ch**ip i**tch** **th**e **th**ing

arm ne**ck**

tr**ee** funn**y** dr**y** dri**ve**

s**a**m**e** r**ai**ny d**ay**

st**o**n**e** c**oa**t t**oe** s**o** elb**ow**

c**u**b**e** c**ue** n**ew**

b**oi**l t**oy**

s**aw** **or**

h**er** b**ur**n b**ir**ch

kn**ee** **wr**ite br**igh**t

e**dge** pa**ge** sta**tion** fen**ce**

42

Tricky letters and words

The words on the next few pages
[werds]

have letters that are tricky,
[hav]   [ar]

silent

or weird.
[weerd]

oo

With **oo** as in b**oo**t

f**oo**d	s**oo**n	t**oo**	shamp**oo**
m**oo**d	sp**oo**n	b**oo**	kangar**oo**
		c**oo**	
h**oo**t	c**oo**l	z**oo**	ball**oo**n
r**oo**t	p**oo**l		bab**oo**n
r**oo**m	sch**oo**l [scool]		
r**oo**f		* t**o** *	

* **to** * : to the zoo, to school;   to go, to play, to say
         [too]   [too]   [t']   [t']   [t']

My mum thinks it's silly to say 'Boo!' to baboons at the zoo.

My dad thinks so too.

When it's hot, I like to keep cool by jumping in a deep pool.

Tricky oo

With oo as in foot

		And:	
book	wool	to	
cook		into	could
hook	good		should
look	wood	today	would
shook		tomorrow	
took		together	

My dad is good at chopping wood,

but I wish he could cook better food.

He should take a good look at my mum's cookbook.

We went to a farm and saw lots of sheep with long wool.

OW

With **ow** as in c**ow**

h**ow**	d**ow**n	br**ow**n	**ow**l
n**ow**	t**ow**n	cr**ow**n	gr**ow**l
w**ow**	cl**ow**n	fr**ow**n	
r**ow**			

Farmer Brown has a dog that growls

if his cows make a noisy row.

He likes barn owls.

On Sunday a clown came to town.

Tricky ow

With ow as in crow

low	blow	blown	own
glow	grow	grown	flown
slow	mow	mown	
snow	show	shown	
	know	known	
row *			

row* : Sit in a **row*** and **row*** a boat, but make a **row**.

Black crows often sit in a row and make a big row.
This can make dogs growl.

In strong winds trees can get blown down.

I like winters with snow.

My mum thinks that I am quite grown up now.

EA

beach   -   **ea** = **ee**, as in 'thr**ee**'

each	sea	cl**ea**n	br**ea**the	[breethe]	**ear**
b**ea**ch	seal	m**ea**n			[eer]
p**ea**ch	seat		h**ea**ve	[heev]	
r**ea**ch	speak		l**ea**ve	[leev]	hear
t**ea**ch	scr**ea**m	cr**ea**m			dear
		dr**ea**m	**ea**sy	[eezy]	n**ea**r
eat	tea		pl**ea**se	[pleez]	y**ea**r
m**ea**t		l**ea**p			
b**ea**t	j**ea**ns	r**ea**l	cr**ea**ture	[creecher]	
tr**ea**t		p**ea**nut			
b**ea**st	r**ea**d				

At the end of summer we went to the beach each day.

We often had ice cream for a treat.

I like to clean the leaves off mum's garden seat

so that she can sit, drink a cup of tea and read to me.

Tricky **ea**

bread - **ea** = **e**, as in 'b**e**d' or 'h**e**r'

dreamt	spread	**jea**lous [j e ll o s]	**hea**rd [herd]
leapt	thread		
meant	instead	meadow [m e dd ow]	learn
breath			learnt
heavy	ready [reddy]	measure	
	already [awlreddy]	[m e zh er]	search
	steady [steddy]		
deaf			
dead		treasure	early
head	breakfast	[tr e zh er]	earth
read*			

* I like my mum to read to me a bit each day in bed.
    [reed]
  Yesterday my dad read to me as well.
    [red]

I eat bread for breakfast but meat for my tea.
For pudding I like peaches and cream.

My sister is jealous of my new jeans.

Mum helped dad heave a heavy load of leaves.

We searched for treasure in a meadow by the sea.

Ea is tricky too in 'great', 'break', 'steak', 'bear' and 'pear'
[grate]   [brake]   [stake]   [bair]   [pair]

OU

Ou as in cl**ou**d

				Say:
l**ou**d	fo**u**nd	**ou**r	h**ou**se	[houss]
pr**ou**d	ro**u**nd	fl**ou**r		
	so**u**nd	s**ou**r	m**ou**se	[mouss]
out	gr**ou**nd			
ab**ou**t		b**ou**nce	bl**ou**se	[blouz]
with**ou**t		co**u**nt	tr**ou**sers	[trouzers]
	ouch	m**ou**ntain	th**ou**sand	[thouzand]
sh**ou**t	cr**ou**ch			
sn**ou**t	p**ou**ch	m**ou**th		
sp**ou**t				

I found a pound on the ground and gave a loud shout:

'Yippee!'

My mum screams if a mouse gets into our house.

A week ago she had a bad throat and no sound came out

of her mouth.

High mountains seem to reach the clouds.

OU with different sounds

This is really tough stuff
[reely]   [tuf]

ou = u		ou = oo		our = or	
	Say:	group	[groop]	your	[yor]
touch	[tuch]	soup		four	
young					
country		you	[yoo]	course	[corss]
				court	
couple	[cupl]	through	[throo]		
double					
trouble		**ought = awt**		and remember:	
					could
rough	[ruf]				should
tough		bought	[bawt]		would
enough	[inuff]	fought			
		brought			
moustache	[mustash]	thought			

My dad has a prickly moustache. Eating soup makes it wet.

I like to touch it, but if I am too rough, he shouts 'Enough!'

Our school has four house groups for sport.

Driving along country roads, you can see lots of cows.

Tricky **o** - not as in *'hot'* or *'dog'*

o spells **u**	**o** spells **oa**	**o** spells long **oo**
of c**u**p	of b**oa**t	of b**oo**t
other [uther]	**o**h [oa]	
an**o**ther	b**o**th [boath]	
br**o**ther		d**o** [doo]
m**o**ther	m**o**st [moast]	
	alm**o**st	tw**o** [too]
s**o**n [sun]	p**o**st	
w**o**n		wh**o** [hoo]
fr**o**nt	d**o**n't [doant]	
M**o**nday	w**o**n't	
n**o**thing	pr**o**gramme [proagram]	and:
w**o**rried		w**o**rd [werd]
once [wunce]	**o**nly [oanly]	w**o**rld [werld]

On Monday my brother broke both his two front teeth.

My mother is now worried, as it may take a long time

for them to grow back again.

Your teeth grow back only once.

So I hope he will not knock them out again.

Tricky **o-e** - not as in *'bone'* or *'home'*

O-e spells **u** (as in c**u**p)

c**o**m**e** [cum]	c**o**v**e**red [cuverd]			
s**o**m**e**	ab**o**v**e** [abuv]		with silent *e*:	
m**o**n**e**y [munny]	**o**n**e** [wun]		g**o**n**e** [gon]	
d**o**n**e** [dun]	d**o**es [duz]			
	d**o**esn't [duznt]			
l**o**v**e** [luv]				
l**o**v**e**d [luvd]				
l**o**v**e**ly [luvly]				

If you come over to my house tomorrow, we can do our homework together.

With a bit of luck, my mum may make us a cake covered in lovely fudge.

She made one yesterday, but it's already gone.

A is often tricky too - not as in 'cat' or 'hat'

a = ar [as in 'car']

ask	[arsk]	answer	[arnser]
basket			
class		after	
fast		half	[harf]
last			
nasty		bath	
pass		father	
past			
		can't	
castle	[carsl]		
		bananas	

Half my class had bananas from the basket that a teacher brought for our picnic in the garden at the castle.

My granny's cat can't run as fast as my cat can.

If I ask a silly question, my father has a silly answer.

Watch *wa* and *all*
[woch]   [wo]   [awl]

wa = wo		all = awl	
	But:	(as in **crawl**)	and:
w**a**nder [wonder]	w**a**g [wag]	**a**ll	**a**ny [enny]
w**a**nt		c**a**ll	m**a**ny [menny]
w**a**s	w**a**gon [wagn]	f**a**ll	
w**a**sh		t**a**ll	
w**a**tch [woch]		w**a**ll	**a**nyway [ennyway]
	w**a**ter [wawter]	w**a**lk [wawk]	
		always [awlways]	

Try not to fall if you crawl along a tall wall above water.

My dog wags his tail if he wants to go for a walk.

You should always wash your hands with soap and water before meals.
[bifor]

Many children get lost wandering off.

Some words have silent letters
[hav]

With *silent e*

are [ar]	have [hav]	uncle [unkl]
were [wer]		
	give [giv]	trolley [trolly]
before [bifor]	given [givn]	
more [mor]		
ignore [ignor]	live [liv]	asked [arskt]
	lived [livd]	
else [els]		washed [wosht]
	every [evry]	
		dressed [dresst]
	travel [travl]	fixed [fixt]

The 'olley' in 'trolley' sounds just like the 'olly' in 'jolly'.

I have to travel to school by bus every day.
I would rather walk.

Don't worry, you will soon learn to read all the words
in which some letters are silent or just a bit odd.

[Doant wurry, yoo wil soon lern tu reed awl the werds
in wich sum letters ar silent or just a bit od.]

56

More silent letters

fam**i**ly	[famly]	d**oo**r	[dor]	b**ea**utiful	[butiful]
fr**ie**nd	[frend]	fl**oo**r	[flor]		
				favo**u**rit**e**	[favorit]
b**ui**ld	[bild]	w**h**at	[wot]		
b**ui**lt	[bilt]	w**h**en	[wen]	diff**e**rent	[difrent]
b**ui**lder	[bilder]	w**h**ich	[wich]		
		w**h**y	[wy]	sud**d**enly	[sudnly]
bisc**u**it	[biskit]				
		who	[hoo]	i**s**land	[iland]

My mum often has tea and biscuits with her favourite

friend who lives next door.

Last week a builder tiled our bathroom floor.

It looks beautiful now that it's done,

much better than before.

Take great care with these
[grate]   [cair]   [thees]

said	[sed]	**full**	the **u**	**strange**	[strainj]	
says	[sez]	**pull**	is like *oo*	**dangerous**	[dainjeros]	
		push	in 'wool'			
great	[grait]	**put**		**magic**	[madjic]	
				giant	[jiant]	
auntie	[arnty]	**flood**	[flud]			
because	[bicoz]			**picture**	[pikcher]	
laugh	[larf]	**climb**	[clime]	**adventure**	[advencher]	
caught	[cawt]	**kind**	[kined]			
fault	[fawlt]	**mind**	[mined]	**dare**	[dair]	
		behind	[behined]	**care**	[cair]	

I wouldn't dare to climb a big tree.

I don't care if this make my friends laugh at me.

Our shopping trolley was so full, we couldn't push or pull it.

A kind lady came to give us a hand.

I like taking pictures of strange things and creatures.

Some letters are just a bit weird
[weerd]

be [bee]	field [feeld]	lie [ly]
he [hee]	thief [theef]	pie [py]
me [mee]		tie [ty]
she [shee]	genie [jeenee]	
we [wee]	believe [beleev]	

we'll [weel]		eight (8) [ait]
we're [weer]		weird [weerd]

even [eevn]	completely [compleetly]	key [kee]
these [thees]	secret [seecret]	
here [heer]		people [peepl]
here's [heerz]		
there [thair]		machine [masheen]
where [wair]		sure [shor]

On our sports day our school field was full of people.
There were far too many to count.

My dad lost the weird key which starts his wood cutting machine.

I hate the number eight. It's too hard to spell.

Now that you have got this far,

you will soon be able to read nearly every book.

Keep going, and you will get better and better at it

and will no longer need much help from anyone.

Try to make sense of what you read

and you will work out even the words that are hard at first.

If you read a lot, bit by bit, your spelling will get better too.

Keep learning and have lots of fun!